Down the

"TAKE A SIP FROM THIS WEIRD AND WONDERFUL COLLECTION OF WORK"

Creative Hats

First published in Great Britain, 2022 by C H Press, a division of Creative Hats.

First published in hardback in Hertfordshire in 2022 by C H Books, an imprint of Creative Hats.

This paperback edition published in 2022.

Cover design by: C H Books/D Pennington

Edited by: Creative Hats

Down the Inkwell

Fantastic Contributors:

Bob Bootman

Lewis Green

Martyn Kempson

Mina

Nicola Warner

Paul Clark

Tina Cooper

Tricia Ramsay

Contents

A Pen in Time

Paul Clark

Extract from upcoming novel 2022

As soon as I cradled the pen in my hands, I felt a percussive beat carry through my body. My mind was clear looking at the discarded Biro, faded yellow pencil a broken sharpener. I closed my eyes, drew in a breath; I could hear a high tide in Winter at the port of Lidburn. I'd spent last Winter there too. I hoped it could release my writer's block.

This pen seemed heavier than its fellows. I turned it in my hands. It seemed to burst into light as the muted beam from the cherry red Anglepoise reflected shades of silver and sapphire contrasting with the dull, matt silver finish.

It was a Golden Wonder crisp box from the local auction. That's where I found it. The pen. The flavour advertised was Worcester sauce, my sister's favourite. We'd got back into the habit of attending auctions as one of our friends, now deceased, first introduced us to the 'community' twenty years ago. I can still recall the buzz in the room on Friday nights as we navigated bargains.

In the box there were a few prints of dhows and trains, but what really drew me to Lot 61 was a compass, 12 inches in diameter, a leather-bound telescope and a small, grease ridden wooden box. I hadn't noticed the pen *that* night.

Always Learning
Tina Cooper

I'm not sure how the conversation began but we ended up talking about our faults. We were taking turns to tell each other how dreadful we truly are.

'William, what are my faults?' I braved.

I knew William wouldn't sugar coat anything, he can't. Think Jim Carrey in Liar Liar.

'Hmmm...'

'Go on William, you know you want to.'

'Well, there's your cooking.'

I just nodded in agreement, it's common knowledge.

'You're kind.'

'That's not a fault William.'

'It is, it annoys me.'

It's true, he has told me this before.

'There's your driving.'

'What's wrong with my driving?'

'It's slow.'

'Again, that's not a fault, it's driving safely. Anything else? You're on a roll.'

'You annoy me.'

So, today I discovered that I still get on William's wick. I've been getting on his wick since he was five and I have the evidence to prove it.

Translation: Dear Mum sumtims you get on my wick Love from William xxx (love heart)

I Learned

Martyn Kempson

Dogs that frighten me
are seldom biting me.
'lovely dog,' I always say
and hope that keeps the brute away.

Always Learning

Paul Clark

Whether teaching or gardening
Studying or conversing
My most important skill
Is to listen rather than to hear
Oh and time does steal
Everything you do
Be authentic, real.

Disney

Nicola Warner

Do not wish upon a star

It's nothing but a lie

Stop worrying where your prince is

No one wants a rat in their kitchen

Everyone has bad days

You are perfect just as you are

Myriad

Lewis Green

M yriad stars that hang above,

Y our head will bear witness to this

R eal life, real time, earth-bound beauty.

I nfinite in fact are they that

A dmire us as we admire them

D rawn down from the night to inspire.

Tears of a Clown

Martyn Kempson

I tried so hard with Tears of a Clown
but my thesaurus let me down.
I could not find a useful noun
to lift my spirts and ease my frown.
I couldn't eat I couldn't sleep
afraid that I might start to weep
morose and miserable I gave a sigh
a little sob and a teary cry.

Essence of Fear

Paul Clark

A scent of fear and liquid fuel
Runs down every road and street
Petrol and diesel very scarce
Amplified heartbeat

Driving from garage to garage
Esso, Tesco and Shell
Hoping to get fuel soon
Everyone is driving pell mell.

Acrid stench and stain of fuel
Pervades each and every day
It hangs in the air
Hopefully it will go away

After a month the crisis halts
People are smiling again
No more shortages
Just the welcome rain.

Amber's Revenge

Nicola Warner

Sophie loved her Amber dolls. It was the first thing she got out in the morning and the last thing her mother made her put away at night. Sometimes she would make her dolls a small bed in the corner of her own so they could have a sleepover.

As Sophie grew, the interest in her dolls slowly faded, replaced with a video game that was infecting the rest of her peers. If you didn't play this game, you were cast out, and she had worked so hard to keep a relationship with her friends, Maddie, Millie and Amy, who she had known since infants.

Maddie was taller than the rest of them, she was slim, with long blonde hair, and vibrant green eyes, she classed herself as the 'leader' or 'queen bee'.

Millie was 2 inches shorter than Maddie, she had brown hair cut to her jaw line, with a natural wave, she was friendly and got excited about everything. Maddie seemed to like her the most.

Amy was short and curvy, with bright auburn hair, she was the quiet one, and very shy around people, but Maddie liked to keep her around, Amy's parents had money and were very generous when they went over to her house.

They were all so eager to grow up. Sophie was still the last to be included in her group.

'Oh, you won't want to go to Sophie's. Her mum still treats her like a baby!' Maddie taunted as they were deciding who would host this week's sleepover.

'She does not!' Sophie defended with a loosely clenched fist.

'She still plays with Ambers!' Maddie whispered to Millie.

'No, I don't!' Sophie stomped her foot.

'Excuse me, I was having a private conversation with Millie.'

'I'll prove it!'

'Fine, let's have the sleepover at yours then, but just remember, I did try to save you the embarrassment, won't you.'

***

'Mum, can I have friends sleep over this weekend?'
'Oh, I don't know...'

'Mum, please! Everyone else has had me stay at their house! Please!'

'Ok, Ok, I suppose it's only fair. Which night?'

'Um ... Friday? No Saturday!'

'Saturday, You're sure?'

'Yes, Saturday," Sophie beamed.

'Saturday it is, we'll order a pizza, sound good?'

Sophie darted at her mum and flung her arms round her waist, 'Thank you, Mum!' and ran off excitedly up the stairs.

Sophie couldn't wait to have her friends stay over, she glanced around her bedroom and gathered up her dolls, which were lined up ornamentally at the back of her chest of drawers, *I should put these under my bed, I don't want to have to deal with Maddie calling me a baby all night,* she told herself. She pushed her duvet up over her bed and opened up her under bed storage drawers. She placed the dolls delicately on top and closed the drawer. She tidied round her room shoving odd bits in drawers that she thought Maddie would make fun of and stood back to take one last glance, *perfect, looks just like anyone else's room,* she told herself proudly.

***

'Sophie! Your friends are here! Come in girls, come in, come in.' Her mother said as she ushered them inside.

'Thank you, Mrs Nightingale!' they responded in unison.

'How are you all? Good?'

The girls nodded their heads.

'Hey guys!' Sophie greeted them as she elephant footed down the stairs.

'Hey Soph!'

'Hi Sophie!'

'Hey, so where do we put our bags?' Maddie asked, faking a smile.

'Oh, you can bring them to my room, come on!'

Maddie scanned Sophie's bedroom with a raised brow, desperately trying to find something to criticise, 'well, I'm impressed Sophie. Not a doll in sight!'

Sophie smiled awkwardly, 'So, erm ... my mum's going to order us pizza, we just need to let her know what we want and when we want it really,' Sophie shrugged with a smile.

'Ooh, Soph, really pushing the boat out, aren't you! Treating us all so special.' Maddie winked, 'You don't fancy one of us, do you?'

'What?'

'Oh, I'm only joking. Come on let's play something while we decide on pizza toppings. Yes?'

The girls nodded in agreement and searched through a pile of board games as Sophie didn't have enough controllers for them all to play Mario Kart together, which Maddie was quick to point out smugly, happy with herself that she had finally found something to criticise.

'Girls! Have you decided on Pizza toppings?' Sophie's mum called.

The girls quickly made their decision after getting side tracked playing Monopoly with Maddie bragging about how many houses she owned.

'Can we have one large plain cheese, one Pepperoni and Mushroom and one Pineapple, please?' Sophie shouted back.

'So, 3 large Pizzas? Are you going to eat all that?'

'Yes! We're starving, Mum!'

'Ok, ok, no problem.' Her mother said in disbelief as she took the phone off the holster to place the order.

'Wow! I can't believe your mum is going to order all that! Mine would have made us share one! You're so lucky!' Millie squealed.

'Just showing off now, aren't you!' Maddie smirked.

'I don't think she's showing off!' Amy stated in defence.

'Oh, gosh Amy, you know, you have been that quiet, I almost forgot you were here!'

'There's no need for that Maddie, you know Amy is shy, give her a break.'

'Oh, Millie, cool it. Amy knows I'm only joking. Right?'

Amy nodded and smiled.

'Shall we finish the game before the pizza gets here? Then we can choose a film to watch while we eat?'

'Yes, lets!' Millie replied.

'Won't take us long anyway,' Maddie boasted, 'None of you can afford to land on one of my houses!' she laughed.

The girls heard the muffled jingle of the doorbell, followed by Sophie's mother thanking, who they assumed was the delivery driver.
'Girls Pizza!' Sophie's mother calls to them, 'You best hurry, before I break my pledge to Slimming World!'
The girls thundered down the stairs.

'Thank you so much, Mrs Nightingale, I'm starving!' Millie squealed.

'Mum, can we take this upstairs and watch a film?'

'I'd rather you didn't eat upstairs, why don't you take it into the front room, you can choose something on Netflix.'

Sophie looked to her friends for guidance.

'I'll stay out of the way, obviously!' her mother continued.

'The sofa would be a lot more comfortable than the floor, Soph.' Amy smiled.

'Grab a plate girls, dig in!' Sophie's mum encouraged them, 'Actually, I'm going to be very naughty and just steal a slice of the cheese pizza, if that's ok?'

'Of course it is, Mum,' Sophie said with a giggle.

'I really shouldn't, but it just smells too good! Don't tell anyone!' She winked and made her way upstairs with her cup of tea, magazine and her sinful slice of pizza, keeping out the way just as she had promised.

The girls loaded their plates and settled on the sofa deciding to watch a romantic comedy and tried not to choke as they laughed through it.

Once the film had finished, they made their way back up to Sophie's bedroom with their belly's swollen and their sides aching from laughter.

'What shall we do now?' Millie asked.

'Let's play Truth or Dare!' Maddie suggested.

'Um ... Ok?' Sophie said.

'I'll start... Sophie, *Truth* or *Dare*?'

'Um ...' Sophie shrugged, 'Truth? I guess?'

Maddie smirked wickedly, 'Where ... are your Amber dolls? I know you still have them!'

'I don't like where this is going.' Amy whispered to Millie, who instantly shushed her.

'Really, Maddie?' Sophie snorted.

'You can always forfeit?' Maddie compromised, smirking.

'You want my dolls? Have them.' Sophie shouted as she threw back her duvet and pulled open the drawer, she reached inside and grabbed Disco Fun Amber and slammed it into, Maddie's hand, 'There, happy?'

Maddie erupted with laughter, 'Oh my god.'

'Should we play another game?' Amy tried to interrupt.

'See Millie, I told you Sophie was a baby. Here's the evidence!' Maddie howled, flicking her long blonde hair back over her shoulder.

'It's not really *that* funny, Maddie.' Amy narrowed her eyes.

'Makes sense you would stick up for her, suppose you want to play with these too?'

'I don't play with them!' Sophie snarled.

'Then why do you still have them?' Maddie questioned, 'Oh my god, you have the alarm clock!' Maddie screamed as she grabbed it out of the drawer, 'Oh this is brilliant, Brit is going to die when I tell her this, oh, it doesn't work, what a shame.' She smirked and tossed it back into the drawer. Brit, short for Britney, was Maddie's older sister, who could be just as cruel than Maddie, if not more, she was the older sister after all, Maddie was just her copycat.

'See. Proof I don't play with any of it.'

'No, that is just proof you ran out of batteries. Oh my god ... how many do you have?'
'Give it a rest, there's only 5 in there.' Sophie rolled her eyes.

'I'm more worried at the fact that there are any are in there at all!'

'Those are the ones my man got for me.'

'Maddie, I think you should stop now, you made your point.'

'No, I haven't.' Maddie peered into the drawer, 'if she wants to keep hanging with us, she needs to prove herself. Don't you, Soph?' Maddie paused and smiled, 'Pull their heads off!' she ordered.

'Maddie!'

'Maddie, stop it!'

Maddie turned to stunned Millie and Amy who were watching open-mouthed, 'She will do it, if she wants to stay in our group,' Maddie turned back to Sophie, 'Ok, not all, just one ... this one.' Maddie pulled out a Amber dressed in a sparkly midnight blue ball gown.

Sophie's eyes filled as she took the doll from Maddie, She had badgered both her Nan and her mum for this one. It was a limited edition, it even came with a stand, it was the only one she had never played with. It was always displayed proudly. It could be worth something one day, it won't be worth anything with a missing head. Sophie stared at it fondly.

'Come on, we haven't got all night!'

Sophie pursed her lips, trying to force her tears back. They escaped quickly down her cheeks, 'fine.' She muttered, and yanked at the dolls head, detaching it from its body with a sharp *pop!* Sophie showed the two parts to Maddie and dropped them back into the drawer.

'Impressive,' Maddie raised her brows in approval, 'Right, what shall we do now? Ooh what about nails? Millie, you do mine. Amy, you're with Sophie.'

'Are you Ok?' Amy whispered.

'I'm fine,' Sophie replied, giving her best reassuring smile.

***

When her friends left the next morning, Sophie pulled out the drawer under her bed and picked out the body and the head of the doll and secured them together with a click, '*I'm sorry*,' she whispered, and placed it down gently beside her. 'Muuuum!'

'Yes, love?'

'Do we have any boxes or black bags, or something?'

'I'll check!'

Her mum came into her bedroom a few minutes later with a small amazon box, 'Is this, ok?'

'Yes, it's just for these dolls, I'm too old for them now, but I'll keep this one.' She smiled and picked up the doll she had just fixed.

'Aww, your Nan, will be happy you're keeping that one, It took her ages to find it.' Her mum smiled and left the room.

Sophie rummaged through the drawer for the other dolls, 'what?' she gasped, 'what the?' Each doll she picked out was missing its head. She rummaged through the draw again, but they weren't there. *'Maddie.'* She growled, *'why didn't she take your head too?'* she asked the doll that she had placed next to her, as she collected the bodies into the box, and buried them with some random bits she found and no longer wanted, or needed, and took the box downstairs.

'Should I put this in the bin outside?' Sophie asked her mother, who was scanning through her Facebook feed.

'Yeah, or you could donate it?'

'Nah, some bits are broken.'

'Bin it is then.'

***

The next morning, she walked to school and met up with her friends, as usual, by the bench under a large drooping tree, its branches draped down around them, creating a little den-like space, which they liked to huddle in.

'Oh my god!' Maddie exclaimed, covering her mouth with her hands, 'You're alive!'

'Of course, I'm alive!' Sophie frowned.

'Well, there's that doll theory debunked.' Maddie sighed.

'What theory?' Sophie narrowed her eyes.

'Of course, you wouldn't know the tale,' Maddie rolled her eyes, 'the curse of the dolls. Legend says that if you mistreat a doll, you know, like you did when you ripped off that poor dolls head? They say that it would come after you when you are safely tucked up in bed. You would hear your name being called first, like ... Sophie ... Sophie ...' Maddie wailed ghost like, wriggling her fingers for effect, 'Then she would tell you where she was, taunting you, pushing you into a state of paralysis... *I'm at the bottom of the stairs ... I'm on the first step ... I'm on the fourth step ... I'm on the tenth step ... I'm on the last step ... I'm by your door ... I'm in your room ... I'm by your bed ... I'm by your head* ...' Maddie walked towards Sophie, 'You wouldn't even have time to make a sound before you heard ... *YOU'RE DEAD!*'

Sophie jumped back as Maddie lunged at her with crooked fingers.

'Aww, is the baby scared?' Maddie taunted and walked away giggling to herself.

***

Sophie struggled to sleep that night. She jumped at every rumble of the boiler and every creak of the floorboards. When she heard her mother make her way to bed, she turned on her bedside lamp, like she used to do when she was 6 to keep her safe from the monster hiding under her bed. Slowly, she drifted into a deep sleep.

***

Britney charged into Maddie's bedroom, 'Come on sissy, rise and shine! Let's start the day with ...

Maddie?'

Maddie's eyes were glazed. She stared blankly in Britney's direction. She didn't acknowledge her sister. She lay there silent. Still.

'Maddie?' she repeated with a broken voice.

Nothing.

'Mum!' she cried hysterically, throwing herself at her sister, shaking her violently, 'Maddie? Maddie! Answer me! Mum! MUM!'

When the ambulance arrived, there was nothing they could do, but they knew that. They announced her dead at the scene and had determined that she had passed some hours ago. As the coroner pushed back Maddie's duvet four dolls' heads tumbled to the floor. The coroner turned to his colleague who displayed the same bewildered look on his face, they found thought it a bit out of the ordinary, but nothing that prompted them to take too seriously. They offered the family their condolences and left with Maddie, hidden under a black zip bag and secured onto a stretcher. Her family watched with their hands clutched over their chests as Maddie was loaded into the van.

***

Hi, I'm Amber! Wake up and let's have some fun today! ... Hi, I'm Amber! Wake up and let's have some fun today! ... Hi, I'm Amb-

Sophie pushed the off button and yawned. She squinted round the room and back around to the alarm clock, her eyes shot open, '*Ok, that's weird, I could have sworn ...*'

'Morning, love.' Her mum said quietly, perching herself at the end of Sophie's bed she wiped the sides of her cheeks with the crook of her finger.

'Are you ok, Mum?'

'Um ... I'm I have just had a phone call ... um ...' she wiped away another tear, 'Oh, honey, I'm so so sorry to have to tell you this, but, um ... Maddie ... She's ... um ... she's died.'

'What? No! Oh my god!' Sophie sat with her hands over her mouth, tears swelling in her eyes.

Hi, I'm Amber! Wake up and let's have some fun today! ... Hi, I'm Amber! Wake up and let's have some fun today! ... Hi! I'm-

Sophie pushed the button to switch the alarm off, assuming to herself that she must have only hit snooze.

'Oh, I'm glad you put that back out, love.' Her mother smiled as she pointed to the doll next to the alarm clock.

Sophie gasped. It was the doll wearing the sparkly purple ball gown, the one that Maddie had chosen for her to behead, the one she had fixed. There.

It was attached to its stand, smiling.

Nope

Tina Cooper

I need to write
But I don't know what
An imagination
I have not got

An autobiography?
Then I needn't think too much
But I haven't done anything
Not yet, as such

Poetry then?
I wrote a corker called Foot
But that was a fluke
And I poem like I cook

What then?
It's just that I feel an urge
I might sit for a bit
Something might emerge

…

Nope

I'm a Nobody

Bob Bootman

I am nothing, I am worthless
Have no value, I am nought
I'm a zero, zilch and zippo
Nothing gained and nothing caught
Sod all, sweet Fanny Adams
Not a sausage, diddly squat
Out for a duck, nill or nada
I have nothing in the pot

Shout Out to my Ex

Tricia Ramsay

When did I say, I wanted a divorce?

I remember saying the home atmosphere had become toxic. With the silent treatment and the passive aggressive behaviour. No eye contact and quick scurrying out of the room if, God forbid, we'd ended up in the same room together. 0 to 60. From not talking to me at all, to being spiteful and nasty for the sake of 'what' exactly?

One of us had to be the adult in this relationship. One of us had to try and think of a solution because burying your head in the sand like an ostrich, even though that's your 'go to mode', isn't helpful, in the long run.

Do you remember the vowels we said to one another? I meant mine ... well not the obey part! That was never going to happen, was it, let's be honest.

That's why I suggested a trial separation. To give ourselves a break. To step back and reflect, what was important to us. How we truly felt about each other. Find out what had changed.

But no, not you, you had to jump in with both feet and say you were filing for divorce and that I was negative and aggressive, even harassing. Reverse psychology, that's what it's called. You were making out *I* was the one who had the problem. You accused me of turning our eldest against you. You did that. ALL by yourself.

You went from 0 to 60. I should have seen it coming, you've got form. But the nastiness, the venomous snarling face, that was new. Over the top and unnecessary. You lose control when you can't control a situation. I had become a 'situation' because I'd had enough and was no longer allowing you to manipulate me.

If anyone had a right to be angry, it should have been me. With years of your controlling and coercive behaviour. I've tolerated that behaviour all this time because I believed in marriage and wanted to keep this family together. In truth we should have separated three years ago when you were horrible on our holiday. You ruined that family holiday. You blatantly flirted with that female hotel employee. I felt embarrassed, not just for my self-esteem but for you. She must have thought you were a right £$%"&! You thought you were it, but in truth, you looked pathetic.

Even our children picked up on the embarrassment and pain you caused me. They could see the tears in my eyes, the betrayal. They could see that you just didn't care. That's what turned your own children against you.

I should be used to you not being able to take responsibility for your actions. You're a coward and I'm long shot of you. You think I need you, can't function without you. Well, all I can say is 'dream on' you pathetic little man. Because I am more than capable. Let's face it, I've been bringing up your kids all their lives, on my own. You have no relationship with them. You sad, sad man.

So go ahead, start hiding our money, remove the money from our joint account and cancel the overdraft without discussion. You can run away, but do you know what? Karma will always catch up with you. You've left me with nothing. I can't afford the cost of a Solicitor. So, I guess I'll need to find an alternative ... something quicker, cheaper and, less time consuming to finally get closure.

Sorry, not sorry.

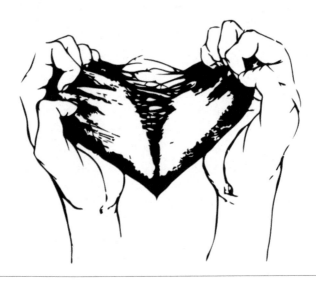

Die please!

Mina

Nazanin enters the quarantine room holding her breath. She knows the smell will be unbearable and tries her best not to breathe for as long as possible. The stench of rotten flesh, however, is beyond any such attempts, it penetrates the mask, turning her stomach and making her retch. Naser looks like a Mummy with his head all bandaged and body covered in white sheets. His only visible eye, which used to soften every time she entered the room, is closed.

For the first couple of weeks after he had shot himself that eye was open and followed her around the room, begging for sympathy or water, communicating pain, brightening a smile when she told him she didn't believe the rumours. Rumours about him abusing a child. The eye crying whenever she begged him to be strong and get better.

That window of communication has been closed for some time now. It is hard for her to imagine any resemblance between this cold, infection - riddled skeleton lying on the bed and her friend Nasser who was a big jolly man full of life. It appears that he had tried to blow out his brain by putting the barrel of his Kalashnikov under his chin. but the shot missed the brain by a fraction, leaving him to suffer with massive and complicated injuries to his respiratory system, his mouth and throat. She moves around the bed checking his blood pressure, his pulse and his breathing. The few remaining detectable signs of life do not bring any joy to her, on the contrary she finds herself upset, even angry. She hates him for prolonging his death and making them all suffer.

'Why can't you just die?' She almost shouts. Then feels guilty about her lack of sympathy. She sits by the bed and holds his hand. The cold touch makes her shudder but she ignores it and softly, almost in a whisper pleads, 'Die my friend. Just let go!'

***

She remembers how she met *Nasser the politician* at a group session. It had been the way he sat, resting his arm on his knee and hunching his shoulders that caught her attention. With his thumb close behind his index and middle finger, he was as if pretending to hold a cigarette or a joint in his hand. She had seen many drug addicted people in her yearlong stay in the city of Kermanshah to recognise that pose. But how could he be a drug addict in a place where even food was hard to come by?

'Why do they call him *Nasser the politician*? He doesn't look like one.' she asked Sabir who was sitting next to her.

'Exactly for that reason...' He whispered, trying to keep a straight face. 'Around here people get nick names for opposite reasons. Look at *little Khalid* for example'

Little Khalid was sitting at the other side of the tent. Six foot and more with broad shoulders and hair sprouting out of every inch of his skin, Khalid was anything but little.

'Ok group let's begin. First, I would like to welcome Comrade Nasser who had joined us today. In the past few weeks we have worked our way through chapter one of Das Kapital. Let's have a recap to help Nasser understand what we have learned so far. Can anyone please give me a summery?' Farid our group leader said and looked around for a volunteer. As the group, collectively, tried their best to explain the complex formula of material + labour = profit, Nazanin occasionally glanced at Nasser to see his reaction. None were detected. He sat in the same position, his face expressionless. Only his deep set, black beetle eyes darted around and focused on whoever was speaking.

'Any questions so far?' asked Farid hoping that the group might have passed on some wisdom.

'Yes' Nasser said finally lifting his dark head. 'That generator out there sure is making a lot of noise. Is there a way we could hold our classes elsewhere?'

***

Nazanin's first guess about Nasser being a drug addict was not far from being correct, only he was a former drug addict who had given up several years back and joined the movement to fight for a better future. He was a handyman, always building or fixing something, walking up and down the camp attending to a cut wire or a broken boiler. Not much of a people's person and usually quiet, it was his skills and his music that made him stand out.

The friendship between Nazanin and him was of a peculiar and unlikely kind. With him being a forty something, coming from a rough background and her a young girl only just turning twenty-one, there was hardly

anything in common between them. Yet they got on very well. He needed someone to appreciate his skills and she wanted to learn new things and hear stories of different kinds of life. They had spent over a month working together, wiring the new hospital building. He taught her about division boxes and negative to positive flow in wires and put her in charge of the generator that provided electricity for the hospital.

Sometimes people made sinister remarks about their friendship or warned her to be careful around him. She couldn't see any reason to be concerned for she had never seen anything but respect and brotherly affection from him. He was a kind-hearted man who was massively misunderstood.

Giving the cold hand a slight squeeze she gets up, finishes her checks and leaves the room in a hurry.

Outside she strips off the white coat, mask, gloves and slippers and runs to the yard to breathe in gulps of fresh, frozen air and shake herself off the smell. Despite piles of snow still refusing to thaw in the corners of the yard, signs of new life could be found from the tiny buds on the branches of the oak tree and the over optimistic cherry tree that was already in full bloom in the middle of February.

'Why are you standing in the cold crying?' Said doctor Azad crossing the yard to check on his patients.

'Please doctor, just help him die. Cut off the oxygen or drips. He has suffered enough and you know there is no hope. We can't help him anymore.' She said wiping her nose with the back of her hand

'I know.' said the doctor sighing heavily 'I have thought about it too, but I can't do that. I am a doctor, it is my duty to help him stay alive for as long as he is hanging there.'

'The most alive things in that room are bacteria that are infesting on him.' she said imagining those microscopic organisms joyfully crawling all over Nasser's body.

The kind doctor touched her lightly on the shoulder and went in, his head hanging in despair.

*Photograph courtesy of Mina

Springtime Feud

Bob Bootman

April was feeling jealous
She started going green
May was filled with colour
Which April found obscene

May also had a maypole
While April just had showers
A couple of Bank Holidays
And longer daylight hours

April thought that May was hot
May thought April cool
There's a May Queen and Mayflower
And she was just an April Fool

Spell for Humanity

Mina

Clear the brain of religion and greed
Make sure you scrub the corners well
As they tend to cling.
Find the draws holding hatred, supremacy, misogyny
And other slimy, stinky elements
Cleanse them thoroughly,
Uproot the weeds that contaminate humanity
Get rid of barbed wires, they keep lovers apart

See how much space you have managed to make

Now, bring in plenty of free thought and reason
Add generous spoonful of science and a pinch of logic
Splash some colours to include everybody
And don't forget to spray several puffs of love

Enjoy your enlarged heart and your new splendid vision!

A Profession

Martyn Kempson

A parking warden
down our road
feet like a hippo
face like a toad.
He stops and sniffs the air
stalks a car and with a glare
he hides inside a nearby thicket
then rushes out and writes a ticket.
This job would suit my twisted brother
he's mean as hell and loves the bother.

Ode to a Barman

Paul Clark

It's easy being a barman
Many people think
But there are some rules
Whilst you hear the glasses chink

Don't talk about politics
Be wary when it's sport
Don't tell your loudest customer
Which team you do support

If you accept a drink
Make sure it's a half an ale
A shandy is alright
Or a mix of mild and pale

Don't tell any jokes
But smile at ones you hear
You're not being paid
To entertain, just serve good beer!

Be friendly and open
Don't ever use a slate
Be smart, never too trendy
And never turn up late.

All Rise

Mina

Chairs were pushed back, robes rustled and wigs were fixed as the court stood up to receive the three magistrates who were going to hear today's case and pass a sentence based on the outcome.

'Ok Mr Murphy you may start with the prosecution's account.' The one in the middle who was wearing a purple sash over his shoulder and across his chest said addressing one of the robed men in the front row.

'Your honour the curious case we are dealing with today belongs to Mr Matthew Palmer a 36-year-old carpenter who loves collecting purses and wallets by stealing them. He has been charged with dishonestly appropriating property belonging to others with the intention of permanently depriving the other person of the belonging. This is in breach of the Theft act 1968 of the criminal offence justice.'

'As my learned friend explained my client has accepted responsibility for his actions and ...'

Listening to the prosecutor and his barrister discussing the particulars of his case and the motivations of his actions, Matthew thought how rigid and detached the law is and how little do these professionals know about the thrills he had experienced getting each purse and discovering what it carried within. It has always amazed him how much one can find out about a total stranger, only by looking through their belongings.

'Mr Palmer, can you come to the witness box please?' Judge's command brought Matthew back to the court. He stood up quickly and walked to where he was directed.

'Mr Palmer, I find your habit or addiction, as your barrister likes to call it, very peculiar indeed. I would like to ask you some questions to help me make sense of your situation. Can you tell me what drives you to pickpocketing?'

'I like purses and wallets Sir.'

'I understand that, but why can't you just go out and buy them. I assume you do have the means to do that.'

'The new purses and wallets have no stories sir, they are characterless.'

'You can get second hand ones too.'

'The second-hand ones are empty Sir. There is no way to guess their stories.'

'Is that what you are after, stories?'

'Yes Sir.'

'What kind of stories have you collected so far?'

'I have had old photographs, love letters, dried flowers, lists and lots of other stuff. I once found a folded napkin in a purse on which a child had written;

Mummy, please don't use lipstick. Remember lipsticks are made of whale fat and we don't want the whales to die. I find these kinds of things interesting.'

'How do you decide whose purse to take?'

'If I find the owner interesting in a way or another or guess that they are the kind of person who carry their memories with them, then I will try to get their wallets or purses.'

'I can imagine most of your victims are older generation.'

'Yes sir, young people these days do not carry pictures of their sweethearts in their wallets. Everything is stored in mobile phones and I find them fake with little sentiment.'

'Once you get a purse what do you do with it?'

'I examine its contents, decide on the kind of story it carries, name it and put it in the special cupboard with a little note.'

'Why do you send the contents back to their owners?'

'To let them know that I am not a thief and I do not intend to misuse their belongings. I even send them some money to compensate for the inconvenience and the loss of the wallet.'

'Do you care about the people you steal from, Mr Palmer?'

'Yes sir, once their stories are revealed to me, it feels like I know them.'

'Mr Palmer, you are an intelligent man. I am sure you do realise that what you have done over the years is theft and it is a serious crime under this country's law.'

'Yes Sir, I know. I am prepared for the consequences Sir.'

'Thank you Mr Palmer. You may sit down.'

As the lengthy and tedious formality of the court went on all day long, Matthew kept an eye on one of the ladies in the room who was sitting on the far right, taking notes. She was one of few court officials with no robes on. He wondered about the kind of story she may have.

Mum: A Blessing

Tricia Ramsay

Wow I can't believe it has been forty years since you had to go away. I remember the evening before, you'd been sleeping most of the day on the sofa. As I was going to bed, I turned to look at you. You opened your eyes and looked straight at me and smiled. That was the last time I saw you.

The confusion. As a ten-year-old. I still went to school that morning. Was tearful at break time because I didn't know whether you had to go back to hospital or had died. Dad hadn't known how to tell me the truth. Not straight away. It wasn't his fault; he'd just lost the love of his life to cancer and was left with three children.

The stress, pain and loss were too great for him, and he followed you a year later.

I think of you every single day. I think what it would have been like, to have had you at my Wedding and your advice and support bringing my children up (although I know you have always been there, in spirit).

I have always spoken about you to my girls and always will.

I love you, miss you, and am always immensely proud to be your daughter.

Although this day will be sad, we will celebrate the amazing woman you were and still are...

Love you, Mum.

*Photograph courtesy of Tricia

Moving On

Tina Cooper

She thought he'd be there in plenty of time, today of all days, boy was he cutting it fine.

Three years she had been waiting for this day, three years of stolen moments and clandestine kisses. She had fallen hard and instantly. Not one to believe in love at first sight she had thought her feelings would fade after a while, once they had been intimate, what would keep them longing for each other, it's the thrill of the chase after all.

Weeks then months passed and still they would seek each other out, long after they had convinced themselves that this would pass and that they mustn't see each other again. They would accidentally find each other at their favourite places, the cafe on the corner of the park, their bench overlooking the city and the book shop where they would leave messages for each other in the copy of Fantastic Writers gathering dust on a shelf at the back. Safer than text messages they thought but mostly because they simply enjoyed the secrecy of it all. Even if a message was found nobody would know who J and W were.

They had talked about what their future would be like if it had been possible for them to have a future. It was more of an in-joke than a plan. They would choose names for their cat, a maine coon with huge feet and a red collar with a bell.

They had talked about where they would live and what car they would buy. They had even chosen the colour of the bedding they would sleep on all the while knowing he wouldn't leave his wife and that they would have to make do with whatever colour their latest hotel room was furnished in.

The longest they had managed to stay away from each other was two months, two painful months. She thought she would cry if she allowed herself to think about it, that couldn't happen again, she'd never survive. She gave herself a telling off. He wouldn't let her down, not now.

His wife's diagnosis had made him feel guilty, they hadn't been happy for years but he had loved her once so he would care for her for as long as he could manage. That was when he had told her they couldn't see each other, that it was over because he wanted to do the right thing. He'd made a promise, for better or for worse. Typical of her to fall for a man with honour albeit a bit fuzzy round the edges. She should move on, he'd said. She'd tried, she'd even been on a few dates, but she was soon checking for messages back at the book shop.

I need to see you. J.

So much for her moving on. She'd chuckled to herself despite feeling nothing but relief.

Their time together became all the more special as caring for his wife was becoming a full-time job. His mother-in-law would give him a day off every now and then but as his wife became weaker the more he felt he should stay home, just in case.

They no longer planned their future, knowing they would get one was enough, their plans could wait.

He'd called her the day his wife died, he'd been crying. They'd been married fifteen years and they'd been happy for the first eight or nine of those. They might have stayed happy if their son had lived, his death had broken both of them and neither had the strength to fix the other.

She'd wanted to go to him but knew she couldn't. No matter, she'd waited this long, she could wait a little longer. They had the rest of their lives ahead of them now.

She looked up at the station clock. He was late, this wasn't like him.

Today was the day. They had settled on Scotland in the end. Far enough to escape their past selves but close enough for people to visit if, or when, they had forgiven them their sins.

They'd had fun house hunting in the highlands and had chosen a small cottage next to Loch Broom. It needed a little work but they would be mortgage free and couldn't wait to get started.

Where was he? She tried his mobile again. It was a man's voice but not her man.

'Who is this?' she asked.

She explained that she was the phone owner's fiancé. It felt so good being able to say it out loud at last.

The man told her he was sorry. A drunk driver apparently, there was nothing anyone could have done. He then asked if it would be possible for her to identify the body. The man began explaining where she needed to be but she couldn't hear him over the screams from the crowd and the screech of the brakes as the driver tried in vain to stop the train.

***

Party Politics

Bob Bootman

I'm very fucking tired
I cannot get to sleep
I've tried herbal medication
And also counting sheep

I went to bed at half past nine
And now it's just gone one
There's a party at the neighbour's
And they're having lots of fun

I didn't get an invite
Because I am a bore
The music's getting louder
It keeps going on 'til four

I'm complaining to the neighbour
It cannot go all night
He's been drinking and he's angry
He wants to start a fight

I said fighting me won't solve this
I need to go to bed
He agreed with me whole heartedly
Then punched me in the head

I ended the night by counting stars
Instead of counting sheep
I was laid out for two hours
At least I got some sleep

I Was Not Surprised

Paul Clark

I was not surprised
The neighbours called
We were noisy late last night
But we had to celebrate
We apologized profusely
It was early rather than late

You see we had a visitor
A person you won't believe
He song so many songs
To the last from number one
Bruce the boss visited
The first song *Born to Run*

Not a Surprise
Martyn Kempson

I was not surprised
that the dog was barking.
he must have heard the old car parking.
It was just like he was talking
"Hurry up its time for walking".

Surprise
Martyn Kempson

A big old cat I loved just went missing
No more scratching, clawing or hissing.
We searched the garden, garage and the house
found spiders, cobwebs and an old grey mouse.
Then in the woollen drawer among the scarves and
mittens
one old cat and five hungry kittens.

MENOPAUSE

Mina

Mean Spirits gather in you

Eating your joy and inviting blue

Nights are too long, sleep is scares

On turns flashes and brings sweat

Periods stop, but bellies grow

Aren't calories burning too slow?

Unpredicted your vagina is

Sore and tender or ready to please

Enough, enough I need some peace

Blessed Relief

Bob Bootman

Aaaah......relief

An overwhelming sense of relief

Having held it for so long

I am now urinating freely into the pan
Bladder emptying quicker than a James Blunt concert

Startled!
I wake up

Relief

An overwhelming sense of relief

Thankfully

I haven't pissed the bed

Sorry

Martyn Kempson

I don't like driving in my car
so only local and don't go far.
Busy traffic to and fro
I'm always searching where to go.
Not enjoying this driving lark
saw a space and tried to park.
Reversed and crashed into a lorry
told the driver I was sorry.

Martyn Kempson

Pink

Some people avoid the sun
fortunately I am not one.
I take my paper and the post
sit by the pool and slowly roast
I watch the sun begin to sink
as I slowly turn from white to pink.

Green

I don't like liver
and I'm sick on ships.
Not very keen on greasy chips
Can't eat Irish stew
made me barf
all over you.
I don't dress up for Halloween
as my face is nearly always green.

Verdigris

Lewis Green

When I was born I embellished the clothes of merchants as a symbol of their wealth. I became a symbol of envy and the very name of envy was born from me - a green-eyed monster they said.

In lush rainforests animals change their colour to be me just for a brief moment in time to escape their death. I am as youthful as a verdant spring and an ever-lasting symbol of regeneration and rebirth. It is also impossible to separate me from scent – you cannot go to the Mediterranean without smelling me entwined in a mixture of eucalyptus, rosemary, juniper, thyme, sage, lavender, pine, and all manner of earthly shrubs.

I am a cool relief against the dry heat, and dragonflies hover in the warm air above lily pads coloured in my hue. Even the lush vegetation of paradise is saturated with me. I have cloaked the Mona Lisa to keep her pale shoulders warm as a gentle breeze rustles around her.

As verdigris you can see me on coins that have passed through many hands over many centuries. Sticky coins that have bartered for all manner of earthly things. You can see me on the hulls of ships that float ceaselessly in the murk, shipwrecked and ghostly. I am the colour of the papyrus plant picked by the Egyptians to scrawl their hieroglyphs, so I can even claim that language evolved because of me.

Balance

Mina

'Look Mum, look, the cootlings have finally hatched. Look how cute they are.' My son points to the other side of the lake where a Mummy coot has been, for the past three weeks sitting on her eggs. His excitement is justified as he has been impatient with these cootlings who have been taking their time to hatch.

'Are you sure they are called cootlings?'

'Sure they are. Like baby ducks are called duckling and baby goose are called
goslings.' He says in his usual matter of fact way.

'Well, we don't say moorlings to the moor chicks, do we?'

'They are called cootlings. Trust me Mum.' somehow over the past few months he
has acquired a sense of authority in regard to wildlife.

It is yet another glorious day in mid-May, the sun is shining generously, the winds have swapped places with a gentle breeze and the airplane-free skies are pristine clean.

Weeping willows, white beams and ash trees with varieties of their green rub shoulders
against each other and sway gently in the soft breeze. Yellow irises and purple bellflowers frame the sides of the lake and reflect in the water where the birds are less active.

We are out again observing the wildlife on and around the lakes as we have done every day since the lockdown. My son's obsession with wildlife has been very good reason for us to be outdoors as much as we could. We have spent hours observing the swans gathering twigs to build their nest; have learned that the black birds that spread their wings in the sun to get dried are called cormorants and admired the great crested grabs dancing side by side on the lake. The coot family in particular has been a source of fascination for us. The long weeks it took the eggs to hatch the parents have worked together as a team one sitting on the eggs while the other dived into the lake gathering food. And now they seem to be fussing around their new babies.

'I hope that red kite up there doesn't notice these cootlings.' My son looks up, alerted by the shrill cry of a big, beautiful bird circling the sky.

'Don't worry darling, Mum and Dad coot will look after them' I try to reassure him.

'I am afraid he has already noticed the chicks.' says an almost whispering voice behind me. I turn around and see a middle-aged woman with bright pink, unruly hair and a face mask looking up at the floating kite above us. She was wearing a long flowing summer dress, equally bright in colour and a pattered woolly shawl hangs loose over her shoulders. I am taken aback by her sudden appearance and her soft whispering voice.

'Did you know that only a couple of those little beauties will reach adulthood?'

She flung a graceful hand across the lake gesturing towards the coots. In no time at all she gets into a telling competition with my son of who has seen more interesting wildlife around the park.

'It is refreshing to find young children interested in nature.' this time her tone is much more cheerful and louder. Trying to keep her distance of two meters, she tells my son where to look for the muntjacs and when would be the best time to spot the bats.

'The wild are more visible now that us humans have been forced to keep indoors.'

'Yes' I nod in agreement 'the whole of nature is much happier now that our cars and planes have stopped pumping polluted gas into the air.'

'Nature is taking its revenge on us dear. This is just a start, believe me.'

I know she is right, but I don't want to believe it. It's like if I believe, it will happen. And yet, I know that nature has a way of keeping balance and there is no denying that we humans have long overstepped that balance.

*Photograph courtesy of Mina

Favour

Nicola Warner

Feb: 'Hey mate, couldn't ask for a favour could I?'

Mar: 'Depends - what it is?'

Feb: 'Well, the thing is, I let a storm overrun and its totally thrown me off, I still have cold days to book in, and I overlooked the flurry of snow that was due on the 21st!'

Mar: 'What are you getting at here?'

Feb: 'Well, I was thinking, you have a few days more than I do, so could I pass the cold days over to you? You would really help me out!'

Mar: 'And give spring to April? She already gets Easter! No way. People count on me for the first day of spring, can't do it mate, sorry!'

Feb: 'Oh, come on!'

Mar: 'No!'

Apr: 'What are you two fighting over now?'

Mar: 'Cheeky git wants to palm off the snowstorm he forgot to register!'

Feb: 'I don't see what the big deal is!'

Mar: 'I've got the best sun for the first day of spring this year! I can't open with that then hit people with snow! They want sun!'

Feb: 'Then do it before!'

Mar: 'No! It will push everything back! It takes days to get the temperature up!'

Apr: 'Oh for God's sake you two! ... I'll take it!'

Tef

Bob Bootman

'Tef' is our goalkeeper
Eighth division, Sunday league
He's usually hungover
And suffering with fatigue
He's a bit of a liability
By a bit, I mean a lot
He's never saved a penalty
Or even a single shot
We blame him for our failure
The main reason for our losses
The manager calls him Jesus Christ
As he's no good with the crosses
'Tef' keeps shouting "keeper's ball!"
A statement very bold
There's no chance that he'll catch it
He couldn't catch a fucking cold
It's how he got his nickname
Now everybody understands
'Tef' is short for Teflon
Coz he's got non-stick hands

The Board Game

Nicola Warner

'Look what I've got for us to play tonight!'
   'Ouija board? Are you sure that's safe?'
   'Why? Are you scared?'
   'No!' Abbie shot back defensively.
   'Good. Come on, let's set it up.'
   The girls opened the box carefully, removed the board setting it down on the floor and placed the pointer in the middle.
   'We have to light a candle.' Jamie stated.
   'A Candle? Why?'
   'I dunno. It's what I've seen them do on that ghost hunting show.' Jamie said as they disappeared out of the room, returning a few minutes later with a large candle and a box of matches.
   Jamie closed her bedroom door and propped a chair up against the handle.
   'What are you doing?'
   'If my parents see that, they will freak out. My mum is really superstitious about these things.'
   'Oh, ok.'
   Jamie carefully took a match out of the box and struck it along the side, she stared at the flame as it made its journey down the matchstick.
   'Jamie!'
   Jamie quickly moved towards the candle and lit the wick just before the flame reached the tip of her fingers.
   'Calm down, Abbie. I know what I'm doing.' She gloated as she discarded the charred matchstick back

into the box.

Abbie watched as Jamie sat on the floor in front of the board.

'Abbie, would you switch off the light?'

'What?'

'The light. Can you turn it off?'

'If I turn off the light, how will we see the board?'

'Oh don't be a pansy, look I'll turn on the lamp, ok? Turn off the light.'

Abbie side eyed Jamie as she flicked the light switch and waited for Jamie to keep her word that she would turn the table lamp on.

'Come on Abbie, sit down.'

'Not until you turn the lamp on.'

'Jamie tutted loudly and reached over to tap the touch sensor base of her bedside lamp, it illuminated a small corner of the room. "There. Happy? Come on, sit down.'

Abbie shuffled over slowly and sat down on the floor opposite Jamie and looked down at the board.

'Now what?'

Jamie moved her eyes away from the flickering flame of the candle, 'now we ask questions,' she replied and placed the tips of her fingers on top of the pointer.

Abbie waited. 'Nothing's happening.'

'You need to put your fingers on it too. Come on.'

Abbie moved her hand hesitantly towards the pointer and placed her fingers on it, as Jamie had done. The pointer jerked underneath their fingers making them shriek.

'Put your finger back on the pointer Abbie, we can't break the connection. And you can't leave the board until it says goodbye, ok?'

Abbie nodded silently and placed her fingers back in position.

The pointer rolled towards the top of the board.

Hello

Their mouths fell open. The girls looked at each other, 'It's working!' Jamie whispered, 'Do you have a message for one of us?'

The pointer moved slowly around the board several times before stopping abruptly.

Yes

Abbie's eye shot up to Jamie, who was staring intently at the board.

'Who do you have a message for?'

Again, the pointer circled the board slowly as if it were pondering the answer, and then shot over towards Abbie.

'Jamie! You're moving that!' Abbie squealed.

'I'm not, I swear!'

'You are! You're trying to scare me!' Abbie cried, snatching back her hand.

'I'm not moving it Abbie, honestly! But we need to keep going, we've opened the door now.'

Abbie placed her fingers back onto the pointer visibly shaking.

'You have a message for Abbie?' Jamie asked the board.

The pointer rotated round the board with a little more speed.

Yes

The pointer moved on, circling the board again, spelling out its message. The girls read the letters out aloud in unison.

" D – I – E "

The colour drained from Abbie's face.

The pointer circulated the board once more...

Goodbye

Cluedo

Martyn Kempson

Invented by a Yank in '49.
Stood the test of time.
Game invented by A Pratt
his real name-fancy that!

American Adventure

Paul Clark

Heading west across the new frontier
Dice in my pocket, a whistle I hear
Arriving at Reading Railroad
A journey I'll make
Too expensive for now
Shanks's pony I'll take
So many avenues, so many places
Connecticut and Virginia, so many faces
Spending time in Marvin Gardens
In this city your frown stone hardens
The end is in sight, this circuit at least
Feet are weary, I'm heading east
Boardwalk or Park Place avoiding the cracks
Darn it! Landed on Luxury Tax!
(Inspired by the American version of Monopoly)

Holidays

Tina Cooper

Holidays are the best, huh? To get away from everything, housework, homework or just work is a joy in itself. The more I tap away the more that word annoys me... work... we need to find a less irritating word for the things we have to do whether we like it or not. Oh dear, just Googled synonyms for *work*, brace yourself.

Toil, labour, drudgery, slog, grind, chores.

big sigh

Anyway.

Holidays are a break from our troubles and from the duties life throws at us. On holiday you can go to bed late and get up at lunch but then have breakfast at lunchtime and lunch at dinner time and then skip dinner and just snack at 11pm just because you can. On holiday you can wear a t-shirt two, maybe three, days in a row because you're unlikely to bump into someone you know so be scruffy just because you can. On holiday you will allow yourself that second slab of cake or have fish and chips more than you should just because you can. On holiday you just can, if you wish.

The best bit about a holiday is that it doesn't even matter where you are. You could be in New York, Magaluf, Sorrento, Hemsby, Scotland or even be at home. Home isn't a first-choice holiday destination but it is still possible to do naff all at Home if you plan it properly. Or, in the case of our most recent Easter break, don't plan at all.

To holiday at Home one must throw caution to the wind. You mustn't eat at the usual times, that is rule no.1. You mustn't go to bed unless you particularly want to and if you want to twice daily then that is ok, it is more than ok in fact, it is preferred. Only do washing when you've all run out of clothes, not a moment before, and never allow the urge to dust or hoover gather momentum. Eat takeout at least once, have chocolate for breakfast as many times as you can stomach it and have a big bag of Doritos with a cold Diet Coke for your elevenses. That's the pm elevenses as, if you're holidaying correctly, you'll still be in bed for the am elevenses.

Of course you don't have to be a lazy bugger to enjoy your break.

You could walk the dog at 6am or 3pm. You could go for a walk and be gone for hours because there's nowhere you need to be. Perhaps, like me, you'll dust off your bike and send it to be serviced only to then pop it back in the shed to gather new dust. It's the thought that counts right? You could watch that Leslie Sansone dvd you asked your mum for a million birthdays ago whilst eating the cake you have had time to bake because you're on holiday.

Ideally you would leave home and disappear to the coast or head up a mountain, less risk of deciding to redecorate or sort the loft. When choosing a holiday you must consider how little work, toil, labour, drudgery, slog, grind and chores you want to do. Don't underestimate the guilt that comes with sitting but ignore it, it's just a week or two.

So, destination is almost irrelevant but the who you holiday with is very important.

Some wise soul once said "it's not where you are, it's who you're with" or something equally as profound and they couldn't have been more of a smart arse if they'd have tried.

The who can be anyone and may change depending on the destination or activity.

We took the eldest skiing many moons ago, this was not the best idea we've ever had. Turns out he doesn't enjoy moving much. We once ended up taking both children to the Goodwood Revival because our babysitter (my mum) was poorly. I had a blast that weekend but our friends, who didn't have children with them, did not. I'm sure it's a coincidence that we've not been invited again.

So. Your travel, or not, companions must be chosen wisely.

I will always choose the kids and The Husband, they are my favourite people. Whether I'm off to the beach or a castle or the top of the garden I will always choose the kids.

All that said, I have discovered another type of holiday.

Ironically my work has become a mini break from it all. At work I wander about an historic garden, water the plants, feed the resident peacocks and chat to visitors. What I cannot do at work is feed the family, walk the dog, put washing on or fill a dishwasher. I also come home from work to a dinner that I haven't cooked which is always a bonus as I can't cook. The more I tap away the more that word thrills me... work... we need to find a more interesting word for the thing we do to escape the boring jobs at home. Oh, just Googled synonyms for *work*, brace yourself.

Function, knead, operate, cultivate.

slightly smaller sigh

Ok, they're not great but still, work can be a small holiday from your other boring jobs.

A holiday can be anything you want it to be.

For me going to college on a Wednesday evening is a small but perfectly formed holiday. I get to talk writerly nonsense with other writers and we laugh a lot, too much perhaps as not much work gets done in those few hours. There's also cake. Walking the dog for an extra hour because I've met a friend and we've been nattering and lost track of time, this too is a tiny holiday. Then there's Fridays. I don't do anything on a Friday. I work weekends and am busy during the week with kids and school runs and dog walks and housework so I allow myself Fridays to do nothing at all. I refuse to pick up a cup or pop a plate in the dishwasher. I take the kids to school then walk the dog then... nothing. Five hours of tea, telly and, if I'm feeling particularly lazy, a little snooze.

I Googled the meaning of holiday.

Noun: an extended period of leisure and recreation

So there you have it, time spent doing the things you want rather than the things you must. Could be a week, a day, a morning or twenty minutes but a holiday is a holiday.

Just keep it to yourselves though. When asked "where are you going on holiday this year?" Don't say you're off to the woods or the library, folks might look at you funny.

3 Spirit

Tricia Ramsay

I was glad the trip in the cab was going to take me half an hour. Half an hour to allow me to compose myself and think things through. My mobile had been ringing off and on, several times, but I didn't bother to check. I knew it would be Alex and he was the last person I wanted to hear from. As I got out of the cab, I paid the driver and gave him a big tip as he'd been exceptionally good and concerned about me when I first got in at the airport. I'd explained that I'd just broken up with my boyfriend and that was why I'd been blubbering in the back, but I'd got myself together again as I left.

I walked up the steps to the front of the apartment building and removed my keys from my bag. Once in the lobby, I checked my mailbox, then walked the two flights of stairs to my apartment. Inside, I locked the front door knowing I was going to be on my own. In my mail, there was a note from Kellie to say she and Nathan had gone away for a long weekend.

It felt cold in the apartment. I wasn't sure if it was because the weather outside had turned bad or whether it reflected my insides; cold, sad, and empty. I walked straight into my bedroom then bathroom, undressed and entered the shower. I tried to cleanse away all the hate and hurt from his betrayal. Once the water started to get cold, I got out, dried and dressed into my comfortable joggers and top. I put on the heating and a cardigan! I also made myself a cup of tea then put the TV on and tried to totally ignore the numbness I felt. My phone rang, and I saw it was Alex again, after a few rings it went off. Then I got a text.

> Trudy.............please I know you're angry and hurt right now, but we need to talk about this. This isn't over, I won't let it. Please talk to me.............your Alex

I texted him back

> Alex what do you mean this isn't over, I won't let it. Arrogance is VERY unattractive. You've really hurt me, how could you? You were the one person I thought I could trust.... you've just blown that out of the water.... I feel betrayed

> Trudy I'M SORRY, I miss judged everything, I know I've messed up. BUT the one thing I know for sure, is the way I feel about you. I really need to talk to you face to face. PLEASE say you'll think about it.

I read his last message then threw my phone down on the sofa and drank my tea, ignored the next couple, and watched TV. I must have drifted off to sleep because when I woke, I checked the time on my phone, and it said 7pm. I had 20 missed calls. My mood was rather like the weather outside. There was a storm, with high winds and the rain looked like it was coming across horizontally. By 8pm I heard the intercom buzzer go off for the apartment and I got up and answered it.

'Trudy it's me, please let me come up?' it was him, he was outside.

'Go away Alex.' I said.

'I'm not going anywhere until I've seen you,' he replied.

I chose to ignore him, and I picked up my mobile. The last message he sent was with him saying if he didn't hear from me, he was coming around. The buzzer went again.

'Please, we need to resolve this, plus I'm soaked through. Let me in Trudy.'

I pushed the intercom button, 'Go home Alex, get in your car and go home,' I replied. 'I haven't got the car, I sent it away,' he said.

'Great, just what I need,' I said. I didn't get any reply. Then I heard knocking on my front door, and it made me jump. I looked through the spy hole. I noticed my heartbeat had quickened and I was annoyed with myself because it was him.

I took a deep breath then opened the door. He looked soaked through; his blue eyes burned into me whilst his wet hair dripped rain droplets down his face. He was breathing heavily but I guess he had just run up two flights of stairs. 'How did you get into the building?'

'One of your neighbours let me in. I told you before, the intercom isn't great as a security device. Can I *please* come in?'

'If I say no, would it make any difference.'

He just raised his eyebrows as if to say 'really, are you kidding me.' I looked him up and down, he was soaked all the way through.

'Come in, take your shoes off.' I moved away to allow him in. 'You're soaked through. Get undressed and grab a shower before you catch your death of cold.'

He walked in, as instructed but continued towards the direction of my bedroom…

Novel to be published Spring 2023.

No Fashion Sense

Bob Bootman

I learned today, what I shouldn't say
When I'm asked for my opinion
Should just agree, what's required of me
Fashion's never been my dominion
"Does this suit me?" she said, with glee
Not in my nature to concur
Slightly mad, pointed to the ad
And said, "It looks better on her!"
Her face turned red at what I had said
Looked like she was going to explode
She started to swear, in the shop, right there
I'd upset her, I think that it showed
"I was making a joke, I'm a stupid bloke."
I said in my defence
Although too late, tried to calculate
What to say to recompense?
"You're a vision of beauty, a stunner, a cutie
I'm lucky that I have you
I tried to plug the hole I had dug
When my ex. appeared,
Right on queue
Nothing I'd learned, as my head was turned
I think my wife started to crack
Slapped me round the face, put me in my place
Then walked out and never came back.

The Lighthouse

Lewis Green

The children were always like this on the night before going on holiday. Just like at Christmas. Just like at Easter. They just could not sleep. It was the same when one of them was expecting a visit from the tooth fairy. They would stay up for as long as possible, until the very act of trying to stay awake was the thing that tired them out and sent them finally to sleep.

Claire got out of bed and headed to the children's room. She knew they were awake by the orange glow beneath the door. Lilly was probably reading in bed again, she thought.

'I wasn't doing anything Mummy,' said Lilly as she pulled the covers up to her chin.

'I don't mind you reading, but we have got to get up early in the morning. Try to get some sleep now.'

'Okay.'

Claire turned round to look at her son's bed.

'Where is your brother?'

'He's playing with his torch downstairs again.'

She put on her slippers and headed down the stairs to the living room. She found George standing on top of the sofa holding his torch out in front of him.

'George what on earth are you doing?'

'I'm the lighthouse keeper...I have to stop the

ships from hitting the rocks,' he waved the torch around casting a beam of light onto the living room floor.

'Well, I'm sure the ships will be okay for one night…get upstairs to bed.'

George carried his torch with him everywhere he went, so it was no surprise to Claire that it was the only thing he wanted to carry in the car with him. Lilly had her backpack filled with books and colouring pencils.

They arrived at the coast just after midday and they parked the car and brought out a small picnic to eat on the beach. Lilly ran into the surf and screamed happily at the coldness of the sea against her legs. George stayed on the sand looking out to sea, every so often pointing his torch towards the horizon.

Claire thought that the sea air would tire them out and so they found a coastal path and took the long route back to the car park around the lighthouse. They passed the sheer white cliffs and saw seabirds nesting among the rocks. Some wheeled and floated in the sky above their heads.

'Mummy, can we have a look in the lighthouse?'

'Yes of course we can…we have to go this way.'

George left his torch on the step outside and they all went inside. There was a small gift shop on the ground floor but there didn't seem to be anybody there. The rope giving access to the top of the lighthouse was down and so they walked slowly up the winding staircase, keeping as close to the wall as possible. All along the wall there were picture frames, filled with black and white photos, the glass covered in dust and some of the frames cracked.

'Mummy, look,' George pointed at the very last picture on the wall. They had now reached the top of the lighthouse.

'What is it, honey?'

'That's me.'

'What do you mean George?'

'That's me when I was the lighthouse keeper.'

'George, that's not you. The picture says this was 1917...that's a long, long time before you were born.'

'Mummy...it was when I was an old man and you were just a little girl...do you remember?'

Claire felt the hackles on her neck rise under the collar of her summer dress.

'No, honey...I don't remember.'

'That's okay...I lived here when I was an old man and one night a ship crashed on the rocks out there,' George pointed through the lighthouse window to the rocks below, 'it wasn't my fault, Mummy, but I was very upset so I went to sleep forever downstairs in the basement.'

Claire put her hand to her throat, 'I think we should go back to the car now ... I'm not feeling very well.'

She grabbed the children by the hands and pushed them in front of her down the stairs. When they got outside George pointed at a wooden square cut into the side of the lighthouse, 'look Mummy, that's where I went to sleep ... down there.'

She walked quickly back towards the coastal path

dragging the children behind her. In their hurry they left the torch sitting on the step.

In the car on the way home, George just kept repeating to himself, 'it wasn't my fault...it wasn't my fault...it wasn't my fault...'

A View from a Room

Martyn Kempson

I am a furry little fella
keen on crumbs and mozzarella.
I have lived for quite a while
in my present domicile.
I am , of course, a little mouse
who has the run of the entire? house.
I avoid the cat, of this I'm certain,
the cat can't follow me up the curtain.
I live in drawers and hide in cracks
and don't have to pay the Council Tax!

La Bête

Lewis Green

Extract from upcoming Novel 2022

Some thought him to be called la bête because of his scars. The scars above Galvin's shoulder were purple and smooth where they were lacking of hair. It was believed these scars were from an old arrow wound, and he was given the nickname after he had pulled out the arrow himself. Others thought it was because of his temper. Others still thought it was because in his cups he became a different person entirely. Or he had fought a bear by hand. Or that in the war he had killed thirteen Confederate soldiers single-handedly. It made no difference that he wasn't even born by the time the war was over. Around campfires all across the country, the travellers speculated as to the meaning of the name or whispered amongst themselves here comes la bête.

Timms and Corsair enjoyed the speculation and teased la bête whenever they heard a new version of how the name came about. The travellers sometimes bribed Timms and Corsair with whisky or gin so that they might find the real story behind the name.

John Joel Galvin had never in his life fought a bear, or, to his knowledge, killed any Confederates. It was true that he had been pierced with an arrow, but that was pulled out by Corsair. It was also in his thigh. The scar on his shoulder had been from an accident in his childhood. His brother had pushed him down a well.

'Have you heard of the beast with two backs?' A learned German leaned it, 'from Shakespeare I believe?'

'No, what does it mean?'

'Well...it just means that...wherever we stop near a settlement, young Joel seems to be able to enjoy the company of ladies.'

The men around the fire laugh and drink to his health. The women blush and look in the direction of the man now feeding the horses, unaware of the discussion around the campfire.

Bears did not fear John Joel Galvin, nor were there shallow Confederate graves left in his wake. His temper was moderate and he would ask for help to pull arrow shafts from his body. He was simply a romantic.

Room with a View

Paul Clark

Staring from the ceiling I'm scanning the room below. The parallel lines of floorboards are broken up by a woven fabric mat made up of brown and white micro squares in a repeated geometric pattern. There are a number of panels of differing colours and textures. These humans, it seems, cannot simply rest on their two lower limbs.

There's a black box which , during certain times of the day(and night) throw out colour and sound. The humans are transfixed as though they are inhabiting another world.

A framework of boxes are aligned from floor to ceiling. In these boxes are smaller boxes of a shiny appearance. They seem to hold storage of memories since when the contents are placed in basic machines sound or vision can be enjoyed. The humans laugh and cry. Over the months I have remained here there is clearly a pattern. The humans communicate with each other.

Atop the frame is a representation of a winged creature. Its wings are folded. It seems great creatures lived here millions of years ago but perhaps they are due to return. When the sun rises tomorrow I shall venture outside this cell. I've been here for six earth months. There is much to learn.

I need to find my way back to the world beyond the stars. I miss my kin so much.

Hope my own room with a view of Alpha Centauri is still the same. Ah memories...

Inside the Mushroom Circle

Nicola Warner

'Come on, this way!'

'Where are we going?' Abbie moaned as she followed Jamie blindly into the woodland not far from her home.

'I've got something to show you!'

The girls crunched their way through the overgrown grass, snapping small branches to clear their way. Jamie stopped abruptly as they approached an opening. She peered across the field which had just been turned over for harvest, 'careful. The farmer shoots people who trespass on his field!'

'You are kidding me!'

'Oh relax, we're not going to play in his field.' Jamie smirked turning back towards the trees.

'Here!' Jamie called to Abbie.

Abbie turned round. Jamie was stood staring up at a large tree. Its trunk was rather slim, and looked weak, it wouldn't last 5 minutes if a storm came through it. Around the base of the tree were tiny mushrooms, they made a perfect circle around the roots. Abbie went to prod one with the tip of her shoe.

'I wouldn't do that if I were you!' Jamie warned.

'Why? It's just a mushroom!'

'Don't you think it strange that they form a perfect circle round this particular tree?'

Abbie shrugged, 'Hadn't really noticed.'

'This is where he appears, this is where you prove your worthy!'

Abbie frowned.

'This is where you do it. Inside the mushroom circle.'

'Do what?'

'You know what.'

'But ... I can't!'

'You can! ... You have to!'

Toad's Stool

Bob Bootman

I have never seen a toad wee
Not a jot, one little bit
Also never found a toad's stool
As I've never seen one shit

Smelly

Tina Cooper

I can never tell
My favourite smell
As it is not the rain
Or freshly popped champagne
Oh ok… I'll spill, it's diesel

Smelly

Martyn Kempson

It was a smell she could not place
She wrinkled her nose and covered her face.
At first she thought it might be varnish
enough to make the silver tarnish.
She smelled her father's greasy hat,
she sniffed the bottom of the cat.
She solved the mystery of the awful stinks
It was her brother's can of Lynx.

Gas Leak

Bob Bootman

Is that cabbage that I'm sniffing?
Or the scent of brussel sprouts
Cannot ascertain the awful smell
Or trace its whereabouts
Dad's in his chair and smirking
I think I have a hunch
He's feeling rather flatulent
Coz he had leeks for lunch

Recipe

Paul Clark

Take four musicians of the rock genre. Put them in the proving area for time enough to make their sound and songs resonate with an audience who have been forcibly removed from public settings.

When the proving is complete ensure the audience has had sufficient exposure to the material, including dance moves and chorus knowledge to contribute to the great event.

Ensure the stage is set including large screens with especial detail to amplification.

Audience to have the fore knowledge that bringing lighters to deploy as dusk falls is mandatory.

Mix the atmosphere with liquid refreshment and a good selection of light , hot and cold, snacks in recyclable packaging and pray for good weather.

And enjoy...

Baked Bean Bath

Bob Bootman

I like to have a Baked Bean Bath
Every month or so
A bounteousness of Baked Beans
From countless tins they flow
Fill the bath with Baked Beans
To just below the brim
Illuminate a candle
I like the lighting dim
Slide in very slowly
Into rich tomato sauce
Have to use the best of brands
I'm using Heinz, of course
Don't do it for the charity
Just do it for the crack
I love the feel of Baked Bean juice
Gently running down my back
Bathe inside my Baked Bean Bath
Soak for about an hour
Then finish off my treatment
By jumping in the shower
Makes me feel re-vitalised
I know, in circumspection
Gives me a natural orange glow
Which is great for my complexion

Shepherds Pie

Tina Cooper

Sunny was the day
Hopeful was my mood
Ever thinking of my belly
Perhaps I needed food
Hurry to the kitchen
Eager to be wooed
Rare is the day that my
Diet can be subdued
Shepherds pie is waiting
Pleasure is pursued
I pop it in the oven
Euphoria ensued

Writing

Paul Clark

W riting isn't hard to do

R egular breaks with tea

I ncrease energy with biccies

T ell story after story

I nteresting life stuff

N eighbours' goings on

G etting like Jackanory

You can find other work from fantastic writers on sale at amazon here:

www.creativehats.co.uk

Printed in Great Britain
by Amazon

87416735R00061